Nursery Rhyme Land

Illustrations by Roger Langton

WHSMITH

EXCLUSIVE · BOOKS ·

Simple Simon met a pieman,
Going to the fair;
Says Simple Simon to the pieman,
Let me taste your ware.

Says the pieman to Simple Simon,
Show me first your penny;
Says Simple Simon to the pieman,
Indeed I have not any.

Simple Simon went a-fishing,
For to catch a whale;
All the water he had got
Was in his mother's pail.

Simple Simon went to look
If plums grew on a thistle;
He pricked his finger very much,
Which made poor Simon whistle.

Old King Cole
Was a merry old soul,
And a merry old soul was he;
He called for his pipe,
And he called for his bowl,
And he called for his fiddlers three.

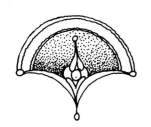

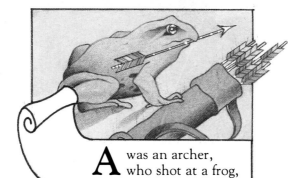

A was an archer,
who shot at a frog,

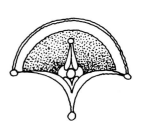

B was a butcher,
and had a great dog.

C was a captain,
all covered with lace,

D was a drunkard,
and had a red fac[e]

E was an esquire,
with pride on his brow,

F was a farmer,
and followed the plough.

G was a gamester,
who had but ill-luc[k]

H was a hunter,
and hunted a buck.

I was an innkeeper,
who loved to carouse,

J was a joiner,
and built up a house

K was King William,
once governed this land,

L was a lady,
who had a white hand.

M was a miser,
and hoarded up gold

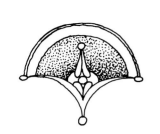

ARCHER

N was a nobleman,
gallant and bold.

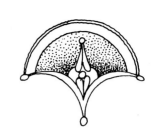

O was an oyster girl,
and went about town,

P was a parson,
and wore a black gown.

Q was a queen,
who wore a silk slip,

R was a robber,
and wanted a whip.

S was a sailor,
and spent all he got,

T was a tinker,
and mended a pot.

U was a usurer,
a miserable elf,

V was a vintner,
who drank all himself.

W was a watchman,
and guarded the door,

X was expensive,
and so became poor.

Y was a youth,
that did not love school,

Z was a zany,
a poor harmless fool.

Mary, Mary, quite contrary,
How does your garden grow?
With silver bells and cockle shells,
And pretty maids all in a row.

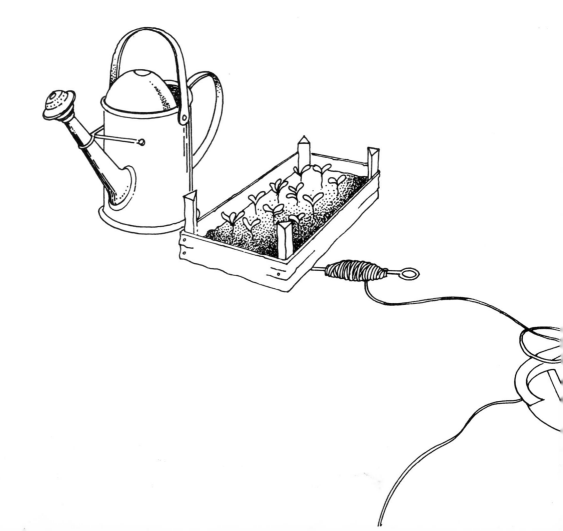

Pat-a-cake, pat-a-cake, baker's man,
Bake me a cake as fast as you can;
Pat it and prick it, and mark it with B,
Put it in the oven for baby and me.

There was an old woman who lived
    in a shoe,
She had so many children she didn't
    know what to do;
She gave them some broth without
    any bread;
She whipped them all soundly and
    put them to bed.

THERE
WAS AN
OLD
WOMAN
WHO
LIVED
IN A
SHOE

The Shoe

The Old
Woman

The Pot

All the Children

Wee Willie Winkie runs through the
town,
Upstairs and downstairs in his night-
gown,
Rapping at the window, crying
through the lock,
Are the children all in bed, for now
it's eight o'clock?

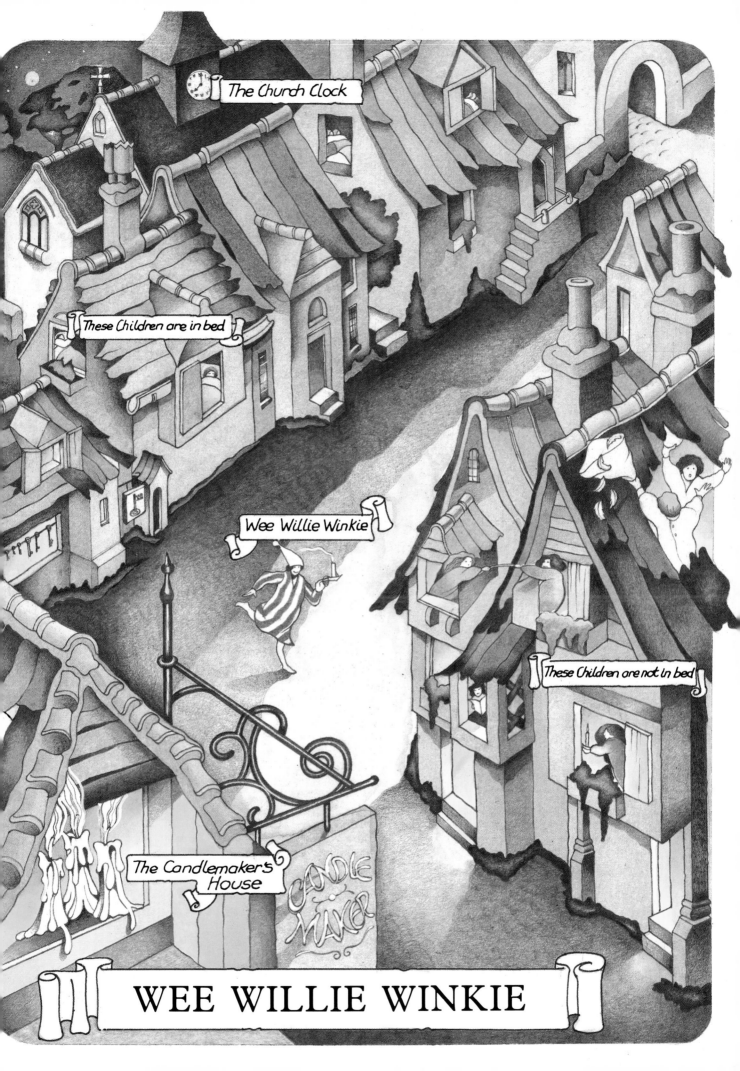

The Church Clock

These Children are in bed

Wee Willie Winkie

These Children are not in bed

The Candlemaker's House

CANDLE MAKER

WEE WILLIE WINKIE

Little Boy Blue,
Come blow your horn,
The sheep's in the meadow,
The cow's in the corn;
But where is the boy
Who looks after the sheep?
He's under a haycock,
Fast asleep.
Will you wake him?
No, not I,
For if I do,
He's sure to cry.

The Cow

The Cornfield

The Meadow

The Farmhouse

The Sheep

Hole in the fence

The Sheep Pen

Little Boy Blue's Horn

The Milking Parlour

LITTLE BOY BLUE

Hickory, dickory, dock,
The mouse ran up the clock.
The clock struck one,
The mouse ran down,
Hickory, dickory dock.

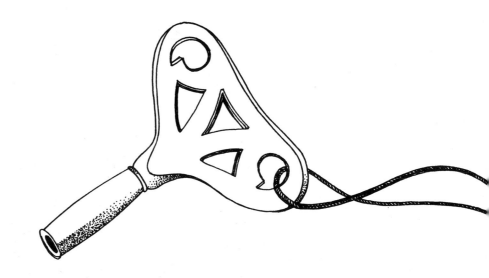

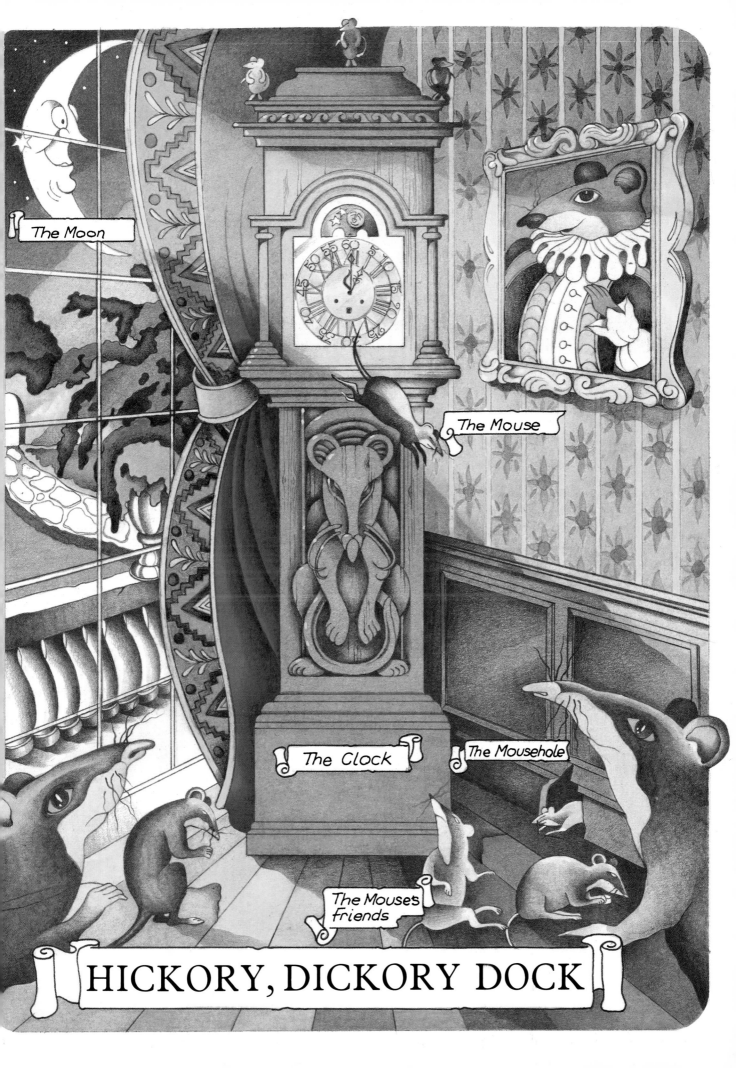

Little Jack Horner
Sat in the corner,
Eating a Christmas pie;
He put in his thumb,
And pulled out a plum,
And said, What a good boy am I!

LITTLE JACK HORNER

Little Jack Horner

The Plum

The Christmas Pie

Christmas Lunch

THIS LITTLE PIG WENT TO MARKET

And this
little pig cried,
Wee-wee-wee-
wee-wee,
I can't find
my way home.

This little pig
had none,

This little pig
went to market,

This little pig
stayed at home,

This little pig
had roast beef,

Jack and Jill
Went up the hill,
To fetch a pail of water;
Jack fell down,
And broke his crown,
And Jill came tumbling after.

Then up Jack got,
And home did trot,
As fast as he could caper;
And went to bed,
To mend his head,
With vinegar and brown paper.

Then Jill came in,
And she did grin,
To see Jack's paper plaster;
Her mother, vexed,
Did whip her next,
For laughing at Jack's disaster.

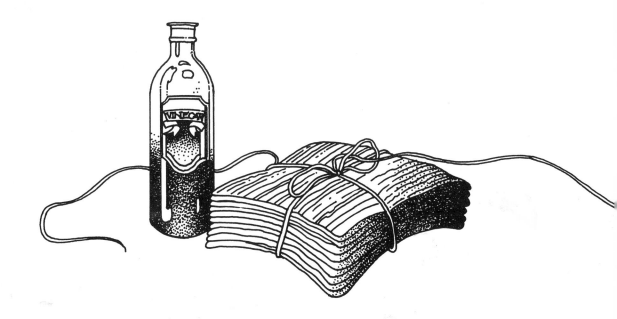

Jack and Jill's House

The Hill

Jill

Jack

Jack in Bed

The Pail of Water

JACK AND JILL

Goosey, goosey gander,
Whither shall I wander?
Upstairs and downstairs
And in my lady's chamber.
There I met an old man
Who would not say his prayers.
I took him by the left leg
And threw him down the stairs.

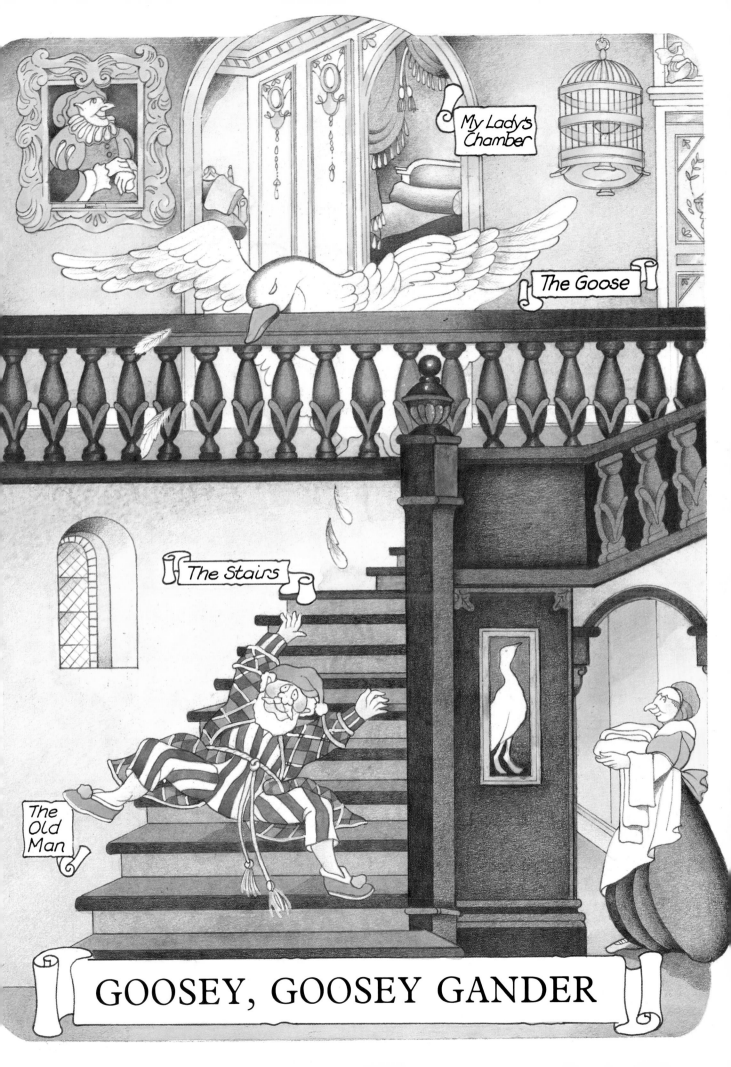

GOOSEY, GOOSEY GANDER

Tom, he was a piper's son,
He learnt to play when he was young,
And all the tune that he could play
Was, 'Over the hills and far away';
Over the hills and a great way off,
The wind shall blow my top-knot off.

Tom with his pipe made such a noise,
That he pleased both the girls and
      boys,
And they all stopped to hear him
      play,
'Over the hills and far away'.
Over the hills and a great way off,
The wind shall blow my top-knot off.

Tom with his pipe did play with such
      skill
That those who heard him could
      never keep still;
As soon as he played they began for
      to dance,
Even pigs on their hind legs would
      after him prance.
Over the hills and a great way off,
The wind shall blow my top-knot off.

TOM, HE WAS A PIPER'S SON

Baa, baa, black sheep,
Have you any wool?
Yes, sir, yes, sir,
Three bags full;
One for the master,
And one for the dame,
And one for the little boy
Who lives down the lane.

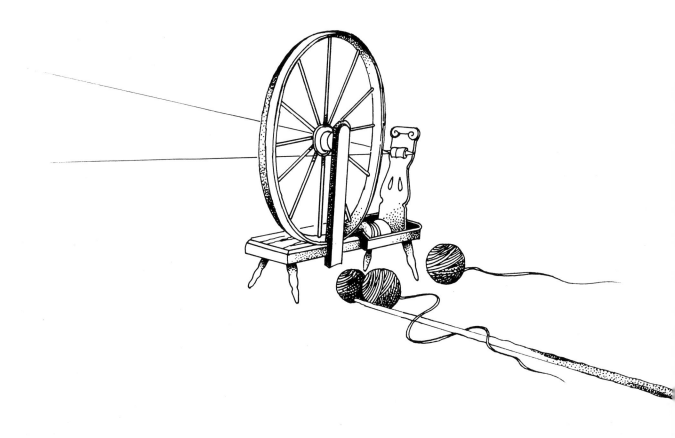

I saw three ships come sailing by,
Come sailing by, come sailing by,
I saw three ships come sailing by,
On New Year's day in the morning.

And what do you think was in them
    then,
Was in them then, was in them then?
And what do you think was in them
    then,
On New Year's day in the morning?

Three pretty girls were in them then,
Were in them then, were in them
    then,
Three pretty girls were in them then,
On New Year's day in the morning.

One could whistle, and one could
    sing,
And one could play on the violin;
Such joy there was at my wedding,
On New Year's day in the morning.

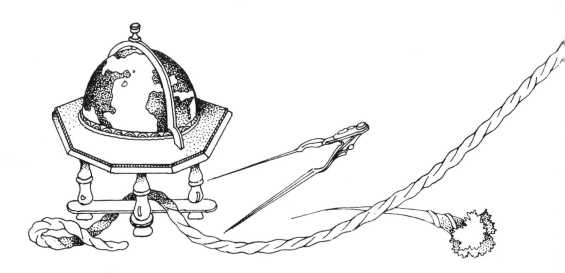

There was an old woman tossed up in
    a basket,
Seventeen times as high as the moon;
Where she was going I couldn't but
    ask it,
For in her hand she carried a broom.

Old woman, old woman, old woman,
    quoth I,
Where are you going to up so high?
To brush the cobwebs off the sky!
May I go with you?
Aye, by-and-by.

THERE WAS AN OLD WOMAN
TOSSED UP IN A BASKET

Sing a song of sixpence,
A pocket full of rye;
Four and twenty blackbirds,
Baked in a pie.

When the pie was opened,
The birds began to sing;
Was not that a dainty dish,
To set before the king?

The king was in his counting-house,
Counting out his money;
The queen was in the parlour,
Eating bread and honey.

The maid was in the garden,
Hanging out the clothes,
Then down came a blackbird,
And pecked off her nose.

The Blackbirds

40

As I was going to St Ives,
I met a man with seven wives,
Each wife had seven sacks,
Each sack had seven cats,
Each cat had seven kits:
Kits, cats, sacks, and wives,
How many were there going to
        St Ives?

AS I WAS GOING TO ST IVES

OLD MOTHER HUBBARD

Old Mother Hubbard
Went to the cupboard,
To fetch her poor dog
a bone; But when
she came there
The cupboard was bare
And so the poor dog
had none.

She went to the baker's
To buy him some bread;
But when she came back
The poor dog was dead.

She went to the undertaker's
To buy him a coffin;
But when she came back
The poor dog was laughing.

44

She took a clean dish
To get him some tripe;
But when she came back
He was smoking a pipe.

She went to the alehouse
To get him some beer;
But when she came back
The dog sat in a chair.

She went to the tavern
For white wine and red;
But when she came back
The dog stood on his head.

She went to the fruiterer's
To buy him some fruit;
But when she came back
He was playing the flute.

She went to the tailor's
To buy him a coat;
But when she came back
He was riding a goat.

She went to the hatter's
To buy him a hat;
But when she came back
He was feeding the cat.

She went to the barber's
To buy him a wig;
But when she came back
He was dancing a jig.

She went to the cobbler's
To buy him some shoes;
But when she came back
He was reading the news.

She went to the seamstress
To buy him some linen;
But when she came back
The dog was a-spinning.

She went to the hosier's
To buy him some hose;
But when she came back
He was dressed in his clothes.

The dame made a curtsy,
The dog made a bow;
The dame said, Your servant,
The dog said, Bow-wow.

47

Blow, wind, blow! and go, mill, go!
That the miller may grind his corn;
That the baker may take it,
And into bread make it,
And bring us a loaf in the morn.

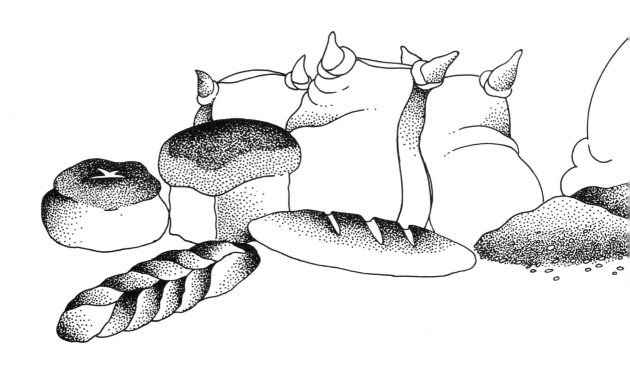

Little Bo-peep has lost her sheep,
And can't tell where to find them;
Leave them alone, and they'll come
    home,
And bring their tails behind them.

Little Bo-peep fell fast asleep,
And dreamt she heard them bleating;
But when she awoke, she found it a
    joke,
For they were still all fleeting.

Then up she took her little crook,
Determined for to find them;
She found them indeed, but it made
    her heart bleed,
For they'd left their tails behind
    them.

It happened one day, as Bo-peep did
    stray
Into a meadow hard by;
There she espied their tails side by
    side,
All hung on a tree to dry.

She heaved a sigh, and wiped her eye,
And over the hillocks went rambling,
And tried what she could, as a
    shepherdess should,
To tack again each to its lambkin.

The lion and the unicorn
Were fighting for the crown;
The lion beat the unicorn
All round about the town.

Some gave them white bread
And some gave them brown;
Some gave them plum cake
And drummed them out of town.

Hey diddle diddle,
The cat and the fiddle,
The cow jumped over the moon;
The little dog laughed
To see such sport,
And the dish ran away with the
spoon.

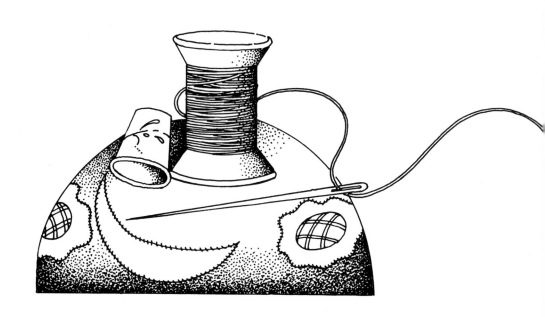

Tom, Tom, the piper's son,
Stole a pig and away did run;
The pig was eat
And Tom was beat,
And Tom went howling down the
        street.

TOM, TOM, THE PIPER'S SON

Mary had a little lamb,
Its fleece was white as snow;
And everywhere that Mary went
The lamb was sure to go.

It followed her to school one day,
That was against the rule;
It made the children laugh and play
To see a lamb at school.

And so the teacher turned it out,
But still it lingered near,
And waited patiently about
Till Mary did appear.

Why does the lamb love Mary so?
The eager children cry;
Why, Mary loves the lamb, you
    know,
The teacher did reply.

MARY HAD A LITTLE LAMB

A farmer went trotting upon his grey
    mare,
Bumpety, bumpety, bump!
With his daughter behind him so rosy
    and fair,
Lumpety, lumpety, lump!

A raven cried, Croak! and they all
    tumbled down,
Bumpety, bumpety, bump!
The mare broke her knees and the
    farmer his crown,
Lumpety, lumpety, lump!

The mischievous raven flew laughing
    away,
Bumpety, bumpety, bump!
And vowed he would serve them the
    same the next day,
Lumpety, lumpety, lump!

BUMPETY, BUMPETY, BUMP

The grand old Duke of York,
He had ten thousand men;
He marched them up to the top of
the hill,
And he marched them down again.
And when they were up, they were
up,
And when they were down, they were
down,
And when they were only half-way
up,
They were neither up nor down.

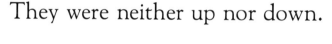

The north wind doth blow,
And we shall have snow,
And what will poor robin do then?
Poor thing.
He'll sit in a barn,
And keep himself warm,
And hide his head under his wing.
Poor thing.

THE NORTH WIND DOTH BLOW

The Queen of Hearts
She made some tarts,
All on a summer's day;
The Knave of Hearts
He stole the tarts,
And took them clean away.

The King of Hearts
Called for the tarts,
And beat the knave full sore;
The Knave of Hearts
Brought back the tarts,
And vowed he'd steal no more.

ONE, TWO
Buckle my shoe

THREE, FOUR
Knock at the door

FIVE, SIX
Pick up sticks

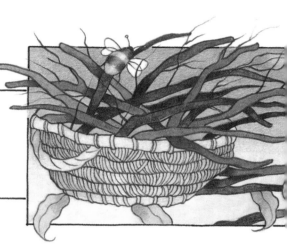

SEVEN, EIGHT
Lay them straight

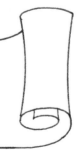

NINE, TEN
A big fat hen

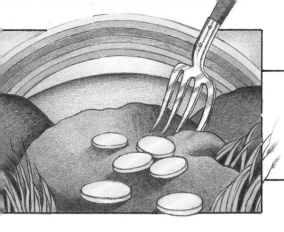

ELEVEN, TWELVE

Dig and delve

THIRTEEN, FOURTEEN

Maids a-courting

FIFTEEN, SIXTEEN

Maids in the kitchen

SEVENTEEN, EIGHTEEN

Maids in waiting

NINETEEN, TWENTY

My plate's empty

Boys and girls come out to play,
The moon doth shine as bright as
    day.
Leave your supper and leave your
    sleep,
And join with your playfellows in the
    street.
Come with a whoop and come with a
    call,
Come with a good will or not at all.
Up the ladder and down the wall,
A half-penny loaf will serve us all;
You find milk, and I'll find flour,
And we'll have a pudding in half an
    hour.

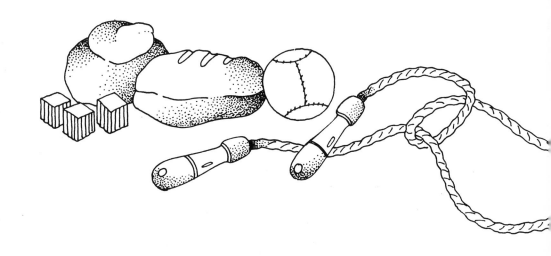

Ride a cock horse to Banbury Cross,
To see a fine lady upon a white horse;
Rings on her fingers and bells on her
    toes,
And she shall have music wherever
    she goes.

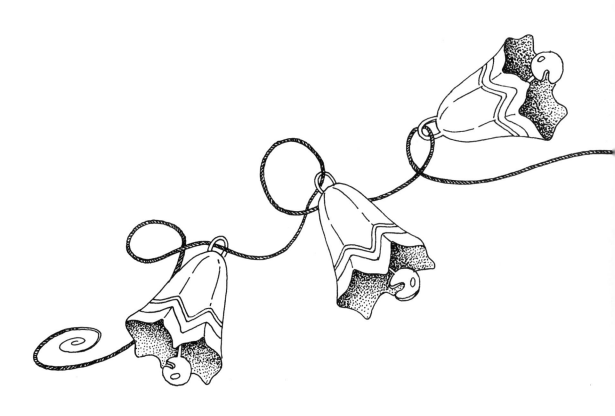

Ipsy wipsy spider
Climbing up the spout;
Down came the rain
And washed the spider out.
Out came the sunshine
And dried up all the rain;
Ipsy wipsy spider
Climbing up again.

IPSY WIPSY SPIDER

Ding, dong, bell,
Pussy's in the well.
Who put her in?
Little Johnny Green.
Who pulled her out?
Little Tommy Stout.
What a naughty boy was that,
To try to drown poor pussy cat,
Who never did him any harm,
And killed the mice in his father's
    barn.

DING, DONG, BELL

Tommy Stout's House

Johnny Green's House

The Well

The Barn

The Mice

Johnny Green

Tommy and Pussy

Two little kittens, one stormy night,
Began to quarrel and then to fight.
One had a mouse and the other had none,
And that's the way the quarrel begun.

'I'll have that mouse!' said the biggest cat.
'You'll have that mouse? We'll see about
    that!'
'I *will* have that mouse!' said the eldest son.
'You shall not have the mouse,' said the
    little one.

I told you before 'twas a stormy night
When these two little kittens began to fight.
The old woman seized her sweeping broom,
And swept the two kittens right out of the
    room.

The ground was covered with frost and
    snow,
And the two little kittens had nowhere to go;
So they laid them down on the mat at
    the door
While the old woman finished sweeping
    the floor.

Then they crept in, as quiet as mice,
All wet with the snow and as cold as ice.
For they found it was better, that stormy
    night,
To lie down and sleep than to quarrel and
    fight.

The Old Woman

Her Broom

The Door

The Mat

The Mouse

The two Kittens

TWO LITTLE KITTENS

I saw a ship a-sailing,
A-sailing on the sea,
And it was deeply laden
With pretty things for me.

There were raisins in the cabin,
And almonds in the hold;
The sails were made of satin,
And the mast was made of gold.

The four and twenty sailors
Who stood upon the decks,
Were four and twenty white mice
With rings about their necks.

The captain was a duck, a duck,
With a jacket on his back;
And when the fairy ship set sail
The captain he said Quack!

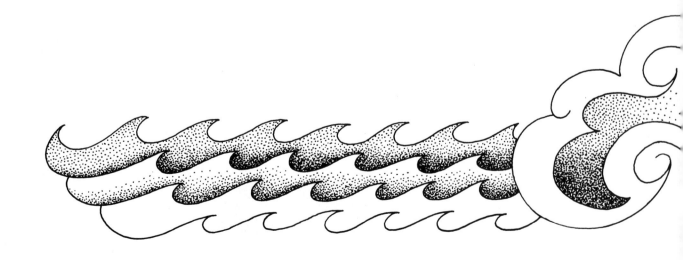

I SAW A SHIP A-SAILING

Humpty Dumpty sat on a wall,
Humpty Dumpty had a great fall.
All the king's horses,
And all the king's men,
Couldn't put Humpty together again.

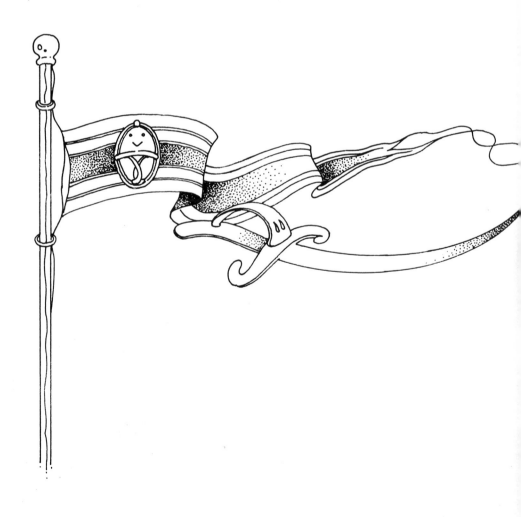

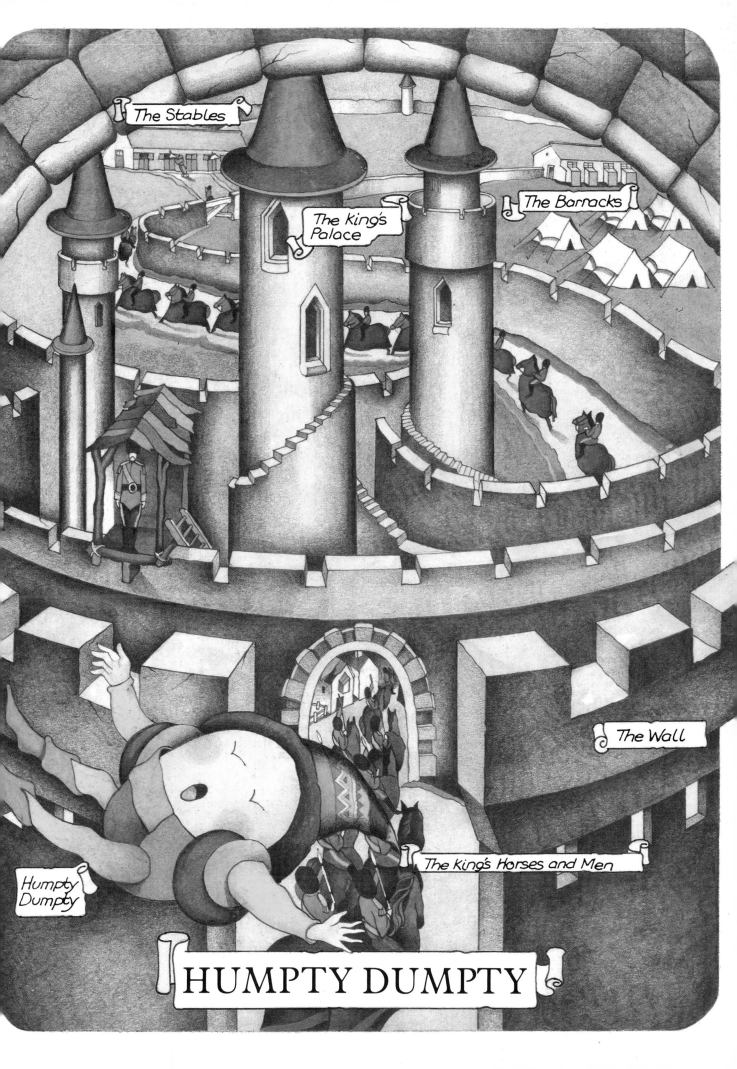

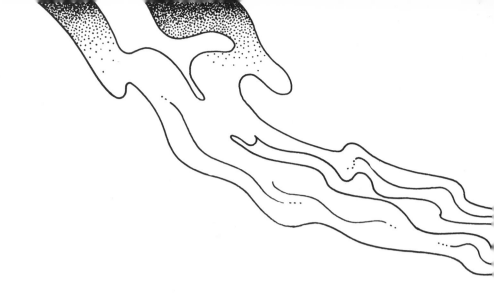

There was a crooked man,
And he walked a crooked mile,
He found a crooked sixpence
Against a crooked stile;
He bought a crooked cat,
Which caught a crooked mouse,
And they all lived together
In a little crooked house.

The man in the moon
Came tumbling down,
And asked his way to Norwich;
He went by the south,
And burnt his mouth
With supping cold pease-porridge.

I had a little nut tree,
Nothing would it bear
But a silver nutmeg
And a golden pear;

The King of Spain's daughter
Came to visit me,
And all for the sake
Of my little nut tree.

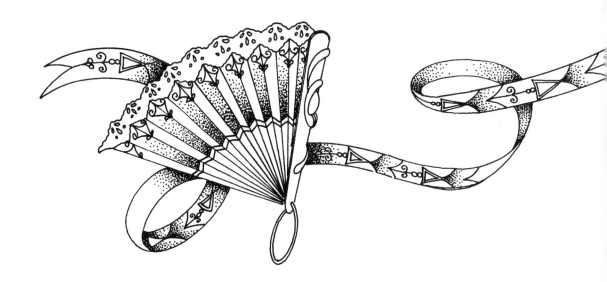

Christmas is coming, the geese are
    getting fat,
Please to put a penny in an old man's
    hat;
If you haven't got a penny a ha'penny
    will do,
If you haven't got a ha'penny, God
    bless you.

CHRISTMAS IS COMING

Twinkle, twinkle, little star,
How I wonder what you are!
Up above the world so high,
Like a diamond in the sky.

When the blazing sun is gone
When he nothing shines upon,
Then you show your little light,
Twinkle, twinkle all the night.

Then the traveller in the dark,
Thanks you for your tiny spark,
He could not see which way to go,
If you did not twinkle so.

In the dark blue sky you keep,
And often through my curtains peep,
For you never shut your eye,
Till the sun is in the sky.

As your bright and tiny spark,
Lights the traveller in the dark, —
Though I know not what you are,
Twinkle, twinkle, little star.

TWINKLE, TWINKLE, LITTLE STAR

The Sky

The Star

The Setting Sun

The Traveller

My Bedroom